FARMSTAND F

Garlic

Over 75 Farm Fresh Recipes

Farmstand Favorites: Garlic
Text copyright © 2012 Hatherleigh Press

Hatherleigh Press is committed to preserving and protecting the natural resources of the Earth. Environmentally responsible and sustainable practices are embraced within the company's mission statement.

Hatherleigh Press is a member of the Publishers Earth Alliance, committed to preserving and protecting the natural resources of the planet while developing a sustainable business model for the book publishing industry.

This book was edited and designed in the village of Hobart, New York. Hobart is a community that has embraced books and publishing as a component of its livelihood. There are several unique bookstores in the village. For more information, please visit www.hobartbookvillage.com.

www.hatherleighpress.com

DISCLAIMER
This book offers general cooking and eating suggestions for educational purposes only. In no case should it be a substitute nor replace a healthcare professional. Consult your healthcare professional to determine which foods are safe for you and to establish the right diet for your personal nutritional needs.

Library of Congress Cataloging-in-Publication Data is available upon request.
978-1-57826-405-6

All Hatherleigh Press titles are available for bulk purchase, special promotions, and premiums. For information about reselling and special purchase opportunities, please call 1-800-528-2550 and ask for the Special Sales Manager.

Cover Design by Nick Macagnone
Interior Design by Nick Macagnone
Cover Photography by Catarina Astrom

10 9 8 7 6 5 4 3 2 1

Printed in the United States

hatherleigh
Improve your life. Change your world.

Acknowledgments

Hatherleigh Press would like to extend a special thank you to Meghan Price and Christine Schultz—without your hard work and creativity this book would not have been possible.

Table of Contents

All About Garlic

Garlic not only possesses a distinctly appetizing taste, but it is also great for your health. As a natural antiseptic, blood cleanser, and blood pressure reducer, garlic has been an important ingredient in medicinal remedies since antiquity. Garlic contains *allicin*, a naturally-occurring compound with antifungal and antibiotic properties. Because the human body does not build a resistance towards this compound, it is more effective in long-term treatment than pharmaceutical drugs. Garlic releases allicin only when crushed or finely chopped. However, cooking (especially in the microwave) inversely affects the medicinal properties of allicin. To get the freshest and most nutrient-rich garlic, be sure to buy it from your local farmstand or farmer's market.

Garlic also promotes cardiovascular health. *Sulfides* within garlic help lower blood pressure. Unlike allicin, the sulfides' effectiveness does not decrease during the cooking process. However, these sulfides are only activated when the garlic is crushed. Garlic also acts as an antioxidant, which prevents the accumulation of LDL (bad) cholesterol in the arteries. These factors all help to reduce the risk of heart attack and stroke.

Due to its vitamin C, selenium, and manganese content, garlic also releases antioxidants which fight cancer-causing free radicals. Studies show that garlic can reduce the chance of developing common cancers like breast and colon cancer.

Not only does garlic play an important role in a healthy lifestyle, but this staple ingredient for both simple and sophisticated cuisine can also be found at your local farmers' market or farm-stand. Due to its versatility, garlic is a key ingredient in many dish-es—many of which you will find in this book!

Garlic comes in three varieties:

- **Common, or Softneck, Garlic** *(Allium sativum)*: Because this type of garlic lasts longest, it is the variety most commonly found in grocery stores. Despite being termed "softneck," common garlic's outer skin is much thicker than that of hard-neck garlic, which increases its shelf life and allows it to be braided.

- **Hardneck Garlic** *(Allium sativum var. ophioscorodon)*: In com-parison to common garlic, hardneck garlic has a thicker neck but thinner skin. These bulbs can be either purple or white, depending on growing conditions.

- **Elephant Garlic** *(Allium ampeloprasum)*: Recently named in 1941, elephant garlic is actually a leek which resembles a large garlic bulb. Although this garlic grows in larger por-tions, it is milder and lacks the health benefits of other garlic varieties.

Storing Garlic

Be sure to store your garlic in a cool, dry place out of direct sun-light. Because garlic needs aeration, garlic keepers (small ceramic jars with small holes) work well.

Never store garlic in a plastic container or in the refrigerator because this will make your garlic soft and moldy. However, garlic can be stored in the freezer; just be sure to first peel off the skin and wrap it in plastic. Also, to avoid botulism, never store garlic in oil.

Braiding is another popular way to store garlic. Braiding your garlic will help it last longer because the stem will ensure the cloves get proper aeration. However, only common (softneck) garlic can be braided.

Be sure to clean your newly harvested garlic. A toothbrush, vegetable brush, or a clean sponge and running water will suffice in removing the dirt. After drying the bulbs in the sun, put them in a cool, dry place out of direct sunlight for five to seven days. Once the skin becomes papery, you can begin braiding.

Begin with three stalks and fold the right stalk over the middle stalk. Then fold the left stalk over the middle stalk (previously the right one). Then add a bulb to each line so that you have six stalks and three lines. Continue to fold the right and left stalks over the middle until you have added all of your bulbs.

Continue braiding until you run out of stalk. Once you are done braiding, use twine to tie the stalks four to five inches above the bulbs. Be sure the twine is secure. You can then tie an extra loop to hang your garlic.

Did you know?

- The earliest documented use of garlic as a medicinal herb is from ancient Egypt.
- Believed to increase physical strength, garlic was eaten by ancient Greek warriors before battle.
- While constructing the ancient pyramids, slaves ate garlic to increase their endurance.
- The **Codex Ebers** (an ancient medical text) prescribed garlic for the improvement of circulation and in treating skin growths.
- The ancient medical practitioners Hippocrates and Dioscorides prescribed garlic for blood and heart conditions, animal bites, abdominal disorders, and cervical cancer.
- Ancient Chinese and Indian medicine used garlic to treat diarrhea, worms, heart conditions, and digestive ailments.
- In Medieval Europe, monks grew garlic to treat constipation.
- The "Four Thieves" was a garlic and vinegar mixture used to prevent the plague.
- Native Americans used garlic in medicinal teas and to treat wounds, burns, and coughing.
- Europeans used garlic to ward off evil spirits (vampires included).

Preparation

Crushed Garlic

Using the broad side of a large knife, press down on a single clove. The clove will break into a couple pieces, and the skin will have separated. Discard skin.

Crushing releases sulfides (which lower blood pressure) and allicin (which serves as an antifungal and antibiotic).

Chopped Garlic

Crush garlic (see instructions above) and continue to cut it with your knife. Once the clove has reached the desired consistency, add a dash of salt to soak up the juices. If you are concerned about your sodium intake, consider mincing garlic with a garlic press instead.

As in crushing, chopping also releases allicin, which results from the reaction between alliin (an amino acid) and allinase (an enzyme).

Minced Garlic

Using a garlic press is the easiest way to mince garlic—no cutting board needed. Garlic presses also save time by catching the skin. Plus, garlic presses are inexpensive and long-lasting.

However, you can also mince garlic without a garlic press. Follow the above directions for crushed garlic, but this time add kosher salt and press the garlic with the broad side of the knife after chopping.

Mincing garlic, meaning that you cannot chop it any further, releases the maximum amount of allicin. This makes mincing arguably the healthiest way to eat garlic. However, the increased sodium from the salt can negate the effects of the allicin, so be careful!

Roasted Garlic

Cut off the top of the bulb, exposing every clove. If you are cooking one blub, place it in the middle of enough aluminum foil to wrap the entire bulb. When cooking multiple bulbs, you can spread them across an aluminum foil-lined baking tray, and top with a drizzle of olive oil and a dash of salt and pepper. Enclose the garlic in the aluminum foil pouch; seal well. Bake at 400°F for 40 minutes or until cloves become soft to the touch. You can also place the topless bulbs upside-down in muffin trays that have olive oil in the bottom. Cover bulbs with aluminum foil, and bake as directed above. Allow to cool before serving.

Roasting eliminates garlic's pungent flavors, transforming it into a softer, sweeter, and nutty paste-like substance. Roasted garlic works well as an appetizer or in many recipes.

Breakfast

Red Pepper Frittata

Serves 4

Ingredients:

2 teaspoons olive oil, divided
½ cup chopped celery
2 garlic cloves, minced
½ teaspoon dried oregano
1 tablespoon grated Parmesan cheese
1 tablespoon chopped, fresh flat-leaf parsley
2 cups egg substitute
2 red bell peppers, chopped
½ cup chopped onions

Directions:

In a large ovenproof frying pan over medium heat, warm 1 tea-spoon oil. Add the red peppers, celery, onions, and garlic; cook, stirring frequently, for 4 to 5 minutes or until tender. Remove from heat and set aside. In a large bowl, lightly whisk together the egg substitute, parsley, oregano, and black pepper. Stir in the vegetable mixture. In the same frying pan over medium heat, warm the remaining 1 teaspoon oil. Add the egg mixture and cook until brown around the edges. Cover the pan and reduce heat to low. Cook for 3 to 4 minutes, or until the eggs are set. Meanwhile, pre-heat the broiler. Sprinkle the frittata with the Parmesan. Place the pan about 5 inches from the heat and broil for 1 to 2 minutes, or until golden brown. Serve cut into wedges.

Skillet Potato and Sausage Hash

Courtesy of Earthbound Farm
(www.ebfarm.com)
Serves 4

Ingredients:

8 ounces Earthbound Farm Organic Heirloom Fingerling
Potatoes cut into ⅓-inch chunks (about 2 cups)

2 tablespoons canola oil

¼ cup chopped yellow onion or 2 shallots, finely minced

2 cloves garlic, minced

2 cooked chicken-apple or pork sausages (sliced, about 8
ounces)

1 (15 oz.) can white beans, drained, rinsed and roughly crushed

1 cup cherry tomatoes

¼ cup minced fresh basil, divided

4 fried eggs (optional)

Red pepper flakes, to taste

Salt and freshly ground black pepper, to taste

Directions:

Place the potatoes in a steamer set over boiling water; cover and
steam until just barely tender (10 to 12 minutes). Remove the
potatoes from the steamer and set aside to cool. Heat the oil in
a large skillet, preferably cast iron, over medium heat. Add the
onions and cook, stirring frequently, until they soften (about 5
minutes). Add the garlic and red pepper flakes, and cook, stirring frequently, for 1 minute. Add the potatoes, sausage, beans,
cherry tomatoes, and half of the basil to the skillet and raise
the heat to medium-high. Cook, stirring occasionally, until a
golden crust forms on the underside (about 10 minutes). Season
with salt and pepper to taste. To serve, divide the hash onto
four plates and top each with a fried egg, if you like. Scatter
some of the remaining basil over each plate and serve hot.

Italian Torte with Chard and Prosciutto

Courtesy of Earthbound Farm

(www.ebfarm.com)

Serves 8

Ingredients:

2 tablespoons olive oil

1½ cups diced yellow onions, ¼-inch cubes

4 cloves garlic, minced

1½ pounds rainbow or Swiss chard, stems removed, leaves cut crosswise into 1-inch ribbons

1 cup grated mozzarella cheese

1 cup grated provolone cheese

1 cup grated Parmigiano Reggiano or Pecorino Romano cheese

½ cup ricotta cheese

2 tablespoons unbleached all-purpose flour

¾ cup heavy whipping cream

4 large eggs

1 cup milk

8 ounces thinly sliced prosciutto ham

Salt and freshly ground pepper, to taste

Directions:

Butter a 9-inch round baking dish or cake pan that is at least
2 inches deep (a classic straight-sided soufflé dish works well).
Cut a circle of parchment paper to fit the dish, place in the bottom of the dish, and butter its top surface. Set aside. Heat the
olive oil in a large skillet (preferably non-stick) and cook the
onions over medium-high heat, stirring frequently, until they
are soft (4 to 8 minutes). Add the garlic and chard. Cover the
skillet and cook until the chard wilts, stirring occasionally (10
to 15 minutes). Season with pepper to taste and set aside. Note
that no salt is needed because the ham and cheeses contribute
enough saltiness to the dish. Combine the mozzarella, provolone,
and Parmigiano or Pecorino cheeses in a bowl. In another bowl,
mix the ricotta with the flour. Stir in the cream. Whisk in the
eggs, one at a time, beating until smooth. Add the milk and a
few grinds of freshly ground pepper and mix well to form a custard. Position a rack in the lower third of the oven and pre-heat
to 350°F. To assemble the torte, spread half of the cheese mixture in a layer on the bottom of the prepared pan. Pour enough
custard into the pan to moisten the cheeses. Arrange half the
prosciutto in a layer on top of the cheese. Arrange half of the
chard on top of the prosciutto layer, and add another layer of
custard to almost cover the chard. Repeat this layering proce-
dure with the remaining ingredients, adding custard to each
layer so that the torte will bind together. Use all of the custard.
Place a round of parchment paper on top of the torte and cover
the pan tightly with a piece of aluminum foil. Transfer the baking dish to the oven and bake for 45 minutes. Remove the foil
and continue baking until the filling pulls away from the side of
the pan and the torte has set in the middle (10 to 20 minutes).
Cooking times will vary depending on the pan you use. To test
for doneness, insert a toothpick or wooden skewer into the center of the torte; it should come out dry. Transfer the torte to a
wire rack and cool for 30 minutes before unmolding. To unmold,
place a plate over the top of the dish and invert the torte onto
the dish gently. Peel the parchment from the bottom of the torte
and serve.

Spicy Spanish Potato Tortillas

Courtesy of Earthbound Farm

(www.ebfarm.com)

Serves 4

Ingredients:

1 pound Earthbound Farm Organic Heirloom Fingerling Potatoes (such as French Fingerling or Russian Banana)

1 tablespoon olive oil

1 medium yellow onion, halved and thinly sliced

1 red or green jalapeño pepper, seeded and very thinly sliced, divided

2 cloves garlic, finely minced

1 teaspoon good-quality curry powder

½ teaspoon ground cumin

½ teaspoon garam masala

1¼ cups halved cherry tomatoes

10 large eggs

¼ cup minced fresh cilantro

Salt and freshly ground black pepper, to taste

Directions:

Peel the potatoes, putting them in a bowl of water as you go to prevent browning. Drain, then place them in a steamer over boiling water. Cover and steam until the potatoes are just tender (about 15 to 18 minutes). Drain, and when cool enough to handle, cut them into ⅛-inch thick slices. Meanwhile, heat the oil in a 9- or 10-inch skillet, preferably cast iron, over medium heat. Add the onion and half of the jalapeño and cook, stirring frequently, until the onion softens and colors (about 10 minutes). Add the garlic, curry powder, cumin and garam masala; cook, stirring constantly for 1 to 2 minutes. Remove the skillet from the heat. Being careful not to burn your fingers, neatly arrange the potatoes in the skillet in several layers, alternating with the tomatoes.

Whisk the eggs in a bowl and then stir in the minced cilantro, salt, and pepper to taste. Pour the egg mixture into the skillet. Return the skillet to the stove and cook over low heat until the egg is almost completely set (about 12 to 5 minutes). Meanwhile, position an oven rack 7 or 8 inches from the broiler and pre-heat on high. Transfer the skillet to the oven and broil until the tortilla is puffed and golden brown (2 to 5 minutes). Remove from the broiler and let the tortilla sit at room temperature for 5 minutes. Sprinkle the remaining jalapeños over the tortilla, cut into 4 wedges, and serve hot or at room temperature.

Purifier Smoothie

Courtesy of Peter McClusky, Toronto Garlic Festival
(www.torontogarlicfestival.ca)
Makes two (8-ounce) servings

Ingredients:

1½ cups water (or coconut water or apple juice)
¾ cup kale, coarsely chopped
1 apple, cored and cut into quarters
¼ cup parsley, coarsely chopped
½ avocado, peeled and pit removed
1-2 garlic cloves, peeled

Directions:

Combine all ingredients in food processor and blend at medium speed for 30 seconds, or longer if a smoother consistency is desired. Serve in 8-ounce glasses.

Note: The parsley used in this recipe will help to eliminate garlic breath.

Garlic Farmers' Boiled Egg with Minced Garlic

Courtesy of Peter McClusky, Toronto Garlic Festival
(www.torontogarlicfestival.ca)

Serves 1

Ingredients:

1 medium-sized egg
1 clove minced garlic
1 teaspoon unsalted butter
Salt (or veggie salt) and pepper, to taste

Directions:

Place the raw egg in a saucepan. Fill the saucepan with cool water to 1 inch above the egg. Cook over medium heat until the water starts to boil. Reduce heat and simmer for 2 to 3 minutes for soft-boiled consistency, five minutes for a medium-boiled egg, or 12 minutes for a hard-boiled egg. Remove the egg with a spoon and serve in an egg cup, small end down.

Slice off the large end with a knife or egg scissors. Add garlic, butter, salt, and pepper and gently mix with egg yolk using a small spoon. Serve with toast.

Omelet with Garlic Greens

Courtesy of Peter McClusky, Toronto Garlic Festival
(www.torontogarlicfestival.ca)
Serves 1

Ingredients:

1 tablespoon unsalted butter
½ cup garlic greens, cut in half lengthwise and chopped
crosswise (use the tender light-coloured part of the greens)
2 eggs, beaten
¼ teaspoon kosher salt
½ teaspoon freshly ground black pepper
¼ cup mushrooms (such as shiitake or button), thinly sliced
¼ cup grated cheddar, American, or Swiss cheese

Directions:

Heat a non-stick or seasoned 6- to 9-inch pan to medium heat
for 1 minute. Add butter (being careful not to let it burn). Add
garlic greens and cook 3-5 minutes. Remove from pan and set
aside. Mix salt and pepper with beaten eggs and add to pan.
Cook until the top begins to set. Add the cooked garlic greens,
mushroom, and cheese. If desired, place a lid on the pan to re-
tain heat and help the top part of the omelet to cook.

Starting from the edge of the pan, use a heat-proof spatula to
fold one-third of the omelet toward the center of the pan and
continue until the omelet is roll-shaped. Tilt the pan over a
warmed serving plate until the omelet slides off the pan onto
the plate. Serve with toast.

Soups & Salads

Garlic Bean Soup
Serves 8

Ingredients:
1 pound dry Great Northern beans
1 quart water
1 quart low-sodium vegetable broth
3 tablespoons olive oil
2 garlic cloves, minced
4 tablespoons chopped parsley

Directions:
Place beans in large soup pot, cover with water and bring to boil. Cook 2 minutes, remove from heat. Cover pot and allow to stand for 1 hour. Drain, discarding the water. Combine beans, 1 quart fresh water, and vegetable broth in slow cooker. Sauté garlic and parsley in olive oil in skillet. Stir into slow cooker. Cover and cook on low for 8-10 hour or until beans are tender.

Pesto Minestrone
Serves 8

Ingredients:
Minestrone:

2 cups coarsely chopped cauliflower (the equivalent of about 2 small heads)

1½ cups chopped zucchini (1-2 medium)

3 (14.5 oz.) cans low-sodium chicken broth

1 (16 oz.) can diced tomatoes, drained

1 cup uncooked elbow macaroni or small pasta shells

3 cups kidney beans or black-eyed peas, drained and rinsed

1 cup sliced carrot

1 cup chopped onion

Pesto:

2 tablespoons olive oil

2 garlic cloves

1 cup fresh, loosely packed basil leaves

1 tablespoon water

Directions:
Minestrone:

In a 5-6 quart saucepan, bring ½ cup water to boil and add tomatoes, cauliflower, onion and carrots; reduce heat and simmer, covered, 10 minutes or until vegetables are tender. Add zucchini, beans, broth, and pasta. Return to a boil, reduce heat, and simmer, uncovered, 10 minutes.

Pesto:

Put all pesto ingredients in food processor or blender and process until very finely chopped. Just before serving, remove soup from heat and stir in pesto.

Curried Date Carrot Soup
Serves 4

Ingredients:
⅔ cup pitted dates
1 onion, chopped
2 stalks celery, chopped
2 cloves garlic, minced
1 tablespoon ginger root, minced or substitute 1 teaspoon ground ginger
1½ tablespoons olive oil
2 tablespoons flour
2 (14 oz.) cans low-sodium chicken broth
2½ cups sliced carrots
1 teaspoon ground cumin
½ teaspoon curry powder
1 pinch cayenne pepper
1 pinch black pepper
1 tablespoon lemon juice

Directions:
Chop dates and set aside. In a heavy saucepan, sauté onions, celery, garlic, and ginger in oil over medium heat for 3–4 minutes or until translucent. Remove from heat and stir in flour. Return to heat and cook for 1–2 minutes, then whisk in chicken broth. Stir in carrots, cumin, curry powder, cayenne, and black pepper. Bring to a boil, reduce heat, cover and simmer 10 minutes, stirring occasionally. Stir in dates and simmer another 5–10 minutes, or until carrots are soft. Remove from heat and purée in a blender or food processor until smooth. Pour back into pan. Stir in lemon juice and return to stove top until thoroughly heated. Spoon into bowls and garnish with a spoonful of yogurt.

Chayote Squash Soup with Cilantro Sour Cream

Serves 6

Ingredients:
Chayote Squash Soup:

1 large onion, chopped
2 garlic cloves, minced
1 tablespoon fresh ginger, minced
4 tablespoons flour
1 medium yellow pepper, sliced
3 large chayote squash, peeled, pitted, and sliced
6 cups vegetable broth, divided
½ cup water cilantro, coarsely chopped (for garnish)

Cilantro Sour Cream:

⅓ cup fat-free sour cream
1 tablespoon finely chopped cilantro
⅓ cup skim milk

Directions:
Chayote Squash Soup:

Spray large saucepan with cooking spray; heat over medium heat until hot. Sauté onion and garlic until tender; about 5 minutes. Stir in flour and ginger and cook over medium heat 2 minutes, stirring constantly. Add squash, pepper, and 2 cups broth to saucepan; heat to boiling. Reduce heat to simmer until squash is tender, 15 to 20 minutes. Process mixture in food processor or blender until smooth; return to saucepan. Add remaining broth and water; continue to heat if serving warm or allow to cool if serving chilled. Drizzle with Cilantro Sour Cream and sprinkle with cilantro.

Cilantro Sour Cream:

In a small bowl, mix sour cream, cilantro and milk until combined.

Butternut and Ginger Soup
· Serves 6

Ingredients:

1 teaspoon mild olive oil

1½ cups chopped onion

3 cloves garlic, crushed

2 teaspoons chopped fresh ginger

1½ pounds (6 cups) peeled raw butternut or other winter squash

½ pound (1 cup) new potatoes, peeled and chopped

1 cup unsweetened 100% apple juice

3 cups water or broth

½ cup skim milk

½ teaspoon salt

Garnish:

½ cup chopped Granny Smith apple

2 tablespoons chopped parsley

Directions:

Heat the oil in a high-sided skillet or large saucepan on medium high. Sauté the onions 3 minutes or until tender. Add the garlic and ginger and cook 1 minute longer. Add the squash, potatoes, 100% apple juice, and water or broth. Bring to a boil. Reduce the heat and simmer 35 to 40 minutes or until very soft. Puree in a blender or processor, in batches, until smooth. Pour back into the pan and stir in the milk and salt.

Bouillabaisse

Serves 6

Ingredients:

4 medium red potatoes (about 1½ pounds)
1½ cups thinly sliced onion
1 cup chopped celery
½ cup dry white wine
¼ cup chopped fresh parsley
1½ tablespoons tomato paste
1 tablespoon olive oil
½ teaspoon dried thyme
¼ teaspoon salt
¼ teaspoon saffron threads
¼ teaspoon pepper
⅛ teaspoon fennel seeds
2 (8 oz.) bottles clam juice
2 garlic cloves, minced
2 lemon slices
1 (14.5 oz.) can no-salt-added whole tomatoes, drained
1 bay leaf
½ pound medium peeled shrimp
¾ pound cod or other lean white fish fillets, cut into 1-inch pieces

Directions:

Pierce potatoes with a fork. Arrange potatoes in a circle on a paper towel in microwave oven. Microwave at high 5 minutes; rearrange potatoes and continue cooking for another 5 minutes. Wrap potatoes in a towel, and let stand 5 minutes. Peel and cube potatoes; set aside. Combine onion and next 15 ingredients (onion through bay leaf) in a 3-quart casserole; stir well. Cover with casserole lid, and microwave at high 5 minutes; stir and continue cooking for another 5 minutes. Stir in potato, shrimp, and fish. Cover and microwave on high 3 minutes or until fish flakes easily when tested with a fork. Discard bay leaf.

Cabbage Soup
Serves 8

Ingredients:
1 pound cabbage, finely shredded
4 celery ribs, sliced
4 carrots, sliced
1 onion, chopped
2 vegetable bouillon, low-sodium
2 garlic cloves, minced
1 quart tomato juice, low-sodium
4 cups water

Directions:
Combine all ingredients in slow cooker. Cover and cook on high for 3-4 hours or until vegetables are tender.

Lentil Soup

Serves 4

Ingredients:

2 teaspoons canola oil
1 large onion, finely diced (about 8 ounces)
1 large carrot, finely diced (about 4 ounces)
2 large celery stalks, finely diced (about 4 ounces)
2 garlic cloves, minced
6 cups chicken stock (low-fat and low-sodium)
1 small ham bone (optional)
3 cups lentils, rinsed (about 12 ounces)
1 bouquet garni
Salt and pepper, to taste

Directions:

Heat the oil in a large pan over high heat. Add the onion and sauté until translucent. Add the carrot, celery, and garlic, and cook for 2 minutes. Add the stock, ham bone (if using), lentils, and bouquet garni, and bring to a boil. Reduce heat, cover, and simmer for 35 minutes. Skim the surface to remove foam as needed. Continue to simmer, uncovered, for 10 minutes to thicken the soup. Remove any fat that may rise to the surface of the soup. Remove the ham bone and bouquet garni. Season with salt and pepper, and serve immediately.

Black Bean Soup with Lime and Cumin

Serves 6

Ingredients:

4 cups cooked black beans
1 tablespoon olive oil
1 tablespoon cumin
1 cup chopped onions
1 cup sliced carrots
½ cup chopped red bell pepper
4 cups low-sodium vegetable stock
¼ cup chopped chipotle chilies (or green chilies)
¼ cup plus 2 tablespoons lime juice
Salt, to taste

Directions:

Heat olive oil in a non-stick or heavy-bottomed frying pan over medium heat. Add cumin, chopped onions, carrots, garlic, and bell pepper; cook slowly until browned. Puree the beans with 4 cups stock in a blender or food processor. Add the vegetable mixture, ½ canned chipotle chilies, ¼ cup plus 2 tablespoons lime juice, and salt to taste. Process until velvety smooth. If the soup is too thick, thin it with more stock. Garnish each serving with a slice of lime floating in the middle and a sprinkling of finely chopped cilantro.

Winter Vegetable Soup
Serves 6

Ingredients:

1 cup chopped onions,
1 sweet potato
2 carrots
1 pound banana or Hubbard squash
1 cup parsnips
2 cloves garlic
1 red bell pepper
2 cups low-sodium, low-fat vegetable broth
1 cup pureed tomato
2 tablespoons lime juice
¼ teaspoon cayenne
1 (10 oz.) package frozen peas
⅛ teaspoon black pepper
1 bunch cilantro sprigs, rinsed or thinly sliced green onions

Directions:

Peel onions and cut into ½-inch-thick wedges. Peel the sweet potato, carrots, squash, and parsnips; cut into ¾-inch pieces. Peel and mince or press garlic. Rinse bell pepper; stem, seed, and cut into ½-inch strips. Cook onions, sweet potato, carrots, squash, parsnips, garlic, and 1 cup of broth in a covered pan for 10 minutes, stirring occasionally. Add a few tablespoons of water if mixture begins sticking to pan. Add 1 more cup of broth, along with the bell pepper, tomato sauce, lime juice, and cayenne to taste. Return to a boil, and then reduce heat. Simmer, covered, until vegetables are tender when pierced, about 12 to 15 minutes. If stew sticks to pan or gets thicker than desired, add more broth as needed. Add peas and stir occasionally until hot, about 2 minutes. Add salt and pepper to taste. Ladle into soup bowls, and garnish with cilantro or sliced green onions.

Tri-Colored Green Split Pea Soup

Courtesy of Hood River Garlic Farm

(www.hoodrivergarlic.com)

Ingredients:

2½ teaspoons vegetable oil

½ onion, chopped

3 carrots, chopped

3 stalks celery, chopped

2 small potatoes, chopped

1 bay leaf

5 cloves garlic, minced

2 cups dried split peas

½ cup barley

1 teaspoon salt

6½ cups water

½ cup parsley, dried or fresh

½ teaspoon dried basil

½ teaspoon dried thyme

½ teaspoon black pepper

Directions:

In a large pot over medium heat, sauté oil and onion until onions are translucent, about 5 minutes. Add water, peas, barley, bay leaf, garlic, salt, and pepper. Bring to boil and reduce heat to low. Simmer 2 hours, stirring occasionally. Add carrots, celery, potatoes, parsley, basil, thyme, and pepper. Simmer 1 hour, or until the peas and vegetables are tender.

Roasted Garlic Soup with Thyme Croutons

Courtesy of Hood River Garlic Farm
(www.hoodrivergarlic.com)
Serves 4

Ingredients:

Soup:

4 heads organic garlic
3 cups milk
1 cup cream
Fresh thyme, to taste
Salt and pepper, to taste
Extra-virgin olive oil, to taste

Croutons:

1 small loaf French bread
Fresh thyme, to taste
Salt and pepper, to taste
Extra-virgin olive oil, to taste

Directions:

Soup:

Coat the garlic with olive oil, salt, and pepper and roast in a 350°F oven until the cloves are golden brown, about 45 minutes. Once the garlic is roasted, cut the head in half (from side to side), exposing all the cloves. Squeeze both halves into a bowl, discarding any skin. Pick out any fiber from the skin. Bring the roasted garlic, milk, cream, and thyme to a simmer. Simmer for 10 minutes. Puree in a blender, and then strain through a very fine mesh sieve. Season with salt and pepper. Serve with thyme, croutons, and a light drizzle of extra-virgin olive oil.

Croutons:

Pre-heat the oven to 350°F. Remove the crust from the bread with a knife. Cut the loaf into very small cubes. Toss the cubes with a small amount of olive oil, fresh chopped thyme, salt, and pepper. Place the cubes on a tray and bake until golden brown, stirring occasionally. Serve while warm.

Flu Fighter Garlic Soup

Courtesy of Peter McClusky, Toronto Garlic Festival

(www.torontogarlicfestival.ca)

Serves 2

Ingredients:

2 tablespoons extra-virgin olive oil
1 medium or large onion, chopped
½ cup carrot, finely chopped
3 cups water or soup stock (either chicken stock or vegetable stock)
2 tablespoons roast garlic puree
4 minced garlic cloves
2 tablespoons chopped fresh parsley
¼ cup chopped fresh shiitake mushroom
1 teaspoon thyme
½ cup lentils
Kosher salt and freshly ground black pepper, to taste

Directions:

Add oil to medium-sized saucepan set to medium heat. Add onions, stirring from time to time. Cook to a deep golden brown color. Add carrots, soup stock (or water), garlic puree, two of the garlic cloves, parsley, mushroom, thyme, lentils, salt, and pepper. Simmer for one hour. One minute before serving, add the two remaining garlic cloves.

Serve in mugs or bowls.

Moroccan Lentil Salad
Serves 4

Ingredients:
1¼ cups uncooked lentils
2½ cups water
3 tablespoons lemon juice
1½ tablespoons olive oil
½ teaspoon thyme
½ teaspoon mint flakes
¼ teaspoon salt
⅛ teaspoon black pepper
1 garlic clove
1½ cups quartered cherry tomatoes
1 cup diced cucumber
1½ cups crumbled reduced-fat feta cheese
1 cup thinly sliced celery
4 cups romaine lettuce leaves

Directions:
Place lentils and water in a large saucepan; bring to a boil.
Cover, reduce heat, and simmer 20 minutes or until tender.
Drain well and set aside. Combine lemon juice, olive oil, thyme,
mint, salt, pepper, and garlic in a medium bowl; stir with a wire
whisk until blended. Add lentils, tomatoes, cucumber, cheese, and
celery to dressing mixture; toss gently to coat. Serve on plates
lined with romaine lettuce.

Artichoke and Roasted Red Pepper Salad with Red Pepper Dressing

Serves 8

Ingredients:

Salad:

8 medium artichokes, prepared and cooked as directed for whole artichokes

3 red bell peppers

Lettuce leaves

½ cup sliced red onion

½ cup sliced black olives

Dressing:

1 bell pepper (roasted), reserved from salad preparation

⅓ cup balsamic vinegar

¼ cup white wine or cider vinegar

2 cloves garlic, minced

1 tablespoon chopped fresh basil or 1 teaspoon crushed dried basil

1 teaspoon chopped fresh rosemary or ½ teaspoon crushed dried rosemary

Directions:

Salad:

Halve artichokes lengthwise; scoop out center petals and fuzzy centers. Remove outer leaves and reserve to garnish salad, or to use for snacks another time. Trim out hearts and slice thinly. Cover and set aside. Place whole bell peppers under pre-heated broiler; broil under high heat until charred on all sides, turning frequently with tongs. Remove from oven; place in a paper bag for 15 minutes to steam skins. Trim off stems of peppers; remove seeds and ribs. Strip off skins; slice peppers into julienne strips. Reserve ¼ of the bell pepper strips to prepare dressing. To assemble salads, arrange lettuce leaves on 8 salad plates. Arrange sliced artichoke hearts, remaining bell pepper strips, red onion and olive slices on lettuce. Garnish with a couple of cooked artichoke leaves, if desired.

Dressing:

In blender or food processor container, place reserved bell pepper strips, vinegars, garlic, basil, rosemary, and sugar. Cover and process until well blended and nearly smooth. Spoon dressing over salads.

Green and Orange Salad
Serves 8

Ingredients:
8 navel oranges
¼ cup minced parsley
2 tablespoons snipped chives
3 tablespoons orange juice
1½ tablespoons olive oil
1 tablespoon Dijon mustard
1 clove garlic, minced
Boston or bibb lettuce

Directions:
Peel and section the oranges, removing all the membranes. Place in a large bowl. Sprinkle with the parsley and chives. In a small bowl, whisk together the orange juice, oil, mustard, and garlic.

Green Bean Potato Salad
Serves 8

Ingredients:

Salad:

1 pound green beans,
with ends cut off
2 pounds red potatoes,
cut into bite-sized pieces
1 cup diced red bell pepper
½ cup chopped red onion

Dressing:

3 cloves garlic, minced
3 tablespoons fresh dill
4 tablespoons balsamic vinegar
3 tablespoons olive oil
1 tablespoon Dijon mustard
Black pepper, to taste

Directions:

Steam green beans in a steamer for 5 to 8 minutes. Cook potatoes in boiling water until tender. Cool green beans and potatoes and place in a bowl. Add onion and bell pepper to the cooled green beans and potatoes; top with dressing.

Dressing:

Mix all ingredients together in a small bowl.

Curried Mustard Greens and Garbanzo Beans with Sweet Potatoes

Serves 4

Ingredients:

2 medium sweet potatoes, peeled and sliced thin
1 medium onion, cut in half and sliced thin
2 medium cloves garlic, sliced
½ cup plus 1 tablespoon low-sodium chicken or vegetable broth
½ teaspoon curry powder
¼ teaspoon turmeric
2 cups chopped and rinsed mustard greens
1 (15 oz.) can sodium-free diced tomatoes
1 (15 oz.) can garbanzo beans, drained
2 tablespoons extra-virgin olive oil
Salt and white pepper, to taste

Directions:

Steam peeled and sliced sweet potatoes for approximately 5-8 minutes. While steaming potatoes, slice onion and garlic. Heat 1 tablespoon broth in 12-inch skillet. Sauté onion in broth over medium heat for 4-5 minutes, stirring frequently, until translucent. Add garlic, curry powder, turmeric, and mustard greens. Cook, stirring occasionally until mustard greens are wilted, about 5 minutes. Add diced tomatoes, garbanzo beans, salt and pepper. Cook for another 5 minutes. Mash sweet potatoes with olive oil, salt, and pepper. If you need to thin potatoes, add a little more broth. Serve mustard greens with mashed sweet potatoes.

Greek-Style Garbanzo Salad
Serves 5

Ingredients:

1½ cups cooked (½ cup dry) or 1 (15 oz.) can garbanzo beans, drained
½ cup thinly sliced red onion
½ cup diced tomato
½ cup chopped green bell pepper
3 tablespoons rice vinegar or apple cider vinegar
2 tablespoons lemon juice

2 teaspoons olive oil
2 tablespoons minced garlic
2 tablespoons chopped fresh parsley
Salt and pepper, to taste

Directions:

Combine all ingredients in a large bowl. Let marinate at room temperature several hours, then refrigerate

Garlic and Herb Lima Bean Salad

Serves 5

Ingredients:

Garlic Herb Dressing:

3 tablespoons olive oil
2 tablespoons chopped green onion
3 tablespoons red wine vinegar
3 cloves garlic, minced or pressed
1 tablespoon fresh minced tarragon or 1 teaspoon dried
½ teaspoon honey
½ teaspoon salt
⅛ teaspoon ground nutmeg

Salad:

5 cups cooked baby lima beans (1¾ cups dry makes about 5 cups cooked)
⅓ cup finely chopped parsley

Directions:

Garlic Herb Dressing:

In a small bowl or shaker jar, combine all ingredients and mix well. Set aside.

Salad:

In a large bowl combine beans, parsley, and Garlic Herb Dressing; mix well. Let stand at room temperature one hour before serving or refrigerate up to 6 hours and bring to room temperature before serving. Refrigerate leftovers.

Caesar Salad

Courtesy of Hood River Garlic Farm
(www.hoodrivergarlic.com)

Ingredients:

1 lemon
1 teaspoon coarse sea salt
3 big cloves garlic
1 tablespoon mayonnaise
Dash of Tabasco sauce
Dash of Worcester sauce
¼ cup grated Parmesan cheese
Salt, to taste

Directions:

In a salad bowl, mash the garlic and salt with a pestle or a large wooden spoon until it forms a paste. Squeeze in the juice of the lemon and mix in with a whisk. Slowly pour in the olive oil and whisk it into the lemon juice. The dressing should be fairly smooth by now. Whisk in all the other ingredients except the cheese. Salt to taste, but remember that the cheese will add salt as well.

When ready to serve the salad, add the greens to the bowl; toss. Sprinkle the cheese and toss again. Add pepper to taste. Serve immediately as the greens will wilt in about ten minutes. The dressing will last in a jar in the fridge for a very long time. For the ultimate garlic experience, make some garlic croutons to top the salad.

Fish & Seafood Entrées

Lime Shrimp Kebobs
Serves 2

Ingredients:
16 large shrimp, uncooked, deveined
3 large limes
2 cloves garlic, crushed and peeled
¼ teaspoon black pepper
2 teaspoons olive oil
2 tablespoons chopped fresh cilantro, cleaned
10 medium cherry tomatoes, rinsed and dried
10 small white-button mushrooms, wiped clean and stems removed

Directions:
In a glass measuring cup, squeeze limes, yielding ¼ cup of juice. Add the garlic, pepper, olive oil, and cilantro and stir. Place the shrimp in a medium bowl and pour the cilantro lime marinade over the shrimp. Let the shrimp marinate for 10 to 15 minutes in the refrigerator (do not let them marinate for more than 30 minutes as the acid of the juice will alter the texture of the shrimp). Alternate cherry tomatoes, mushrooms, and shrimp on four skewers. Grill the skewers over a medium heat for 3 to 4 minutes on each side until the shrimp are just cooked through.

Soba Peanut Noodles with Shrimp

Ingredients:

8 ounces soba noodles or whole-wheat spaghetti
¼ cup natural crunchy peanut butter
4 cups shredded cabbage
2 cups shredded carrots
1 cup edamame, shelled and thawed
1 tablespoons grated fresh ginger
2 garlic cloves, minced
½ cup chicken broth
1 pound shrimp, peeled and uncooked
2 tablespoons hoisin sauce
2 teaspoons chili sauce or 1 teaspoon red chili paste
¼ cup chopped cilantro (optional)
Non-stick cooking spray

Directions:

Cook noodles. Drain and rinse. Set aside in a large mixing bowl. In a small saucepan, combine garlic, ginger, chicken broth, peanut butter, hoisin sauce, and chili sauce. Cook on low heat, stirring until peanut butter is blended. Spray non-stick spray in large frying pan. Add cabbage, carrots, and edamame. Cook for about 5 minutes. Add shrimp and sauce mixture and cook until shrimp turn pink, about 5 minutes. Pour mixture over noodles and mix until noodles are well coated. Top with fresh cilantro (optional) and serve.

Shrimp Pasta in Garlic and Basil Cream Sauce

Courtesy of Cornerstone Garlic Farm

Ingredients:

12 ounces penne or other pasta
1 pound medium shrimp, peeled
10 cloves spicy hardneck garlic, divided
4 tablespoons butter, divided
1 medium shallot, minced
1 cup heavy cream
10-12 basil leaves, minced
1½ cups freshly grated Parmesan, divided
Salt and pepper, to taste

Directions:

Cook pasta as directed on the box. In a small, deep skillet sauté the shrimp and 2 cloves of garlic (pressed) in 1 tablespoon of butter until done. Take shrimp out of the pan and add the rest of the butter. Add 6 more cloves of garlic (pressed) and shallots. Sauté for 3 minutes over low heat. Pour in cream, basil, 1 cup cheese, 2 cloves of garlic (thinly sliced), salt, and pepper. Simmer over low heat, covered but vented, until thickened, 7-10 minutes. Add the shrimp back in the pan, mix with sauce, pour over pasta, and top with remaining cheese and a basil leaf.

Salmon Fillets with Rosemary

Courtesy of the National Aquaculture Association
(www.thenaa.net)
Serves 4

Ingredients:
2 tablespoons rosemary, minced
2 cloves garlic, crushed
½ teaspoon white pepper, ground
1 tablespoon olive oil
⅔ cup breadcrumbs
4 U.S. farm-raised salmon fillets
Salt, to taste

Directions:
Pre-heat the oven to 425°F. Combine the fresh minced rosemary, crushed garlic, and white pepper with the olive oil. Run through a food processor for 30 seconds. Season with salt to taste and finish processing to a paste. In a mixing bowl, combine the paste with the breadcrumbs using a fork. Lightly oil a baking dish and arrange the salmon fillets in the baking dish. Press equal amounts of the breadcrumb mixture onto the top of each fillet. Drizzle olive oil on top of the breadcrumbs. Bake for 10-12 minutes or until cooked throughout.

Note: Black spots on the gill covers distinguish Atlantic salmon from their Pacific cousins.

Clams Casino

Courtesy of the National Aquaculture Association

(www.thenaa.net)

Ingredients:

50 U.S. farm-raised littleneck clams
1 cup white wine
8 slices bacon, fried and crumbled
2 cups breadcrumbs
1 stick butter, melted
3 cloves garlic, minced
¼ cup parsley leaves, chopped
¼ cup Parmesan cheese, finely grated
1 tablespoon salt
1 green pepper, chopped
Hot pepper sauce, to taste

Directions:

Pre-heat broiler. Place the white wine and clams in covered pot and steam until clams have opened. Discard any clams that do not open. Remove the clams from the pot and remove meat from shells. Arrange clams on the half-shell. In a medium bowl, mix the bacon, breadcrumbs, butter, garlic, parsley, Parmesan, salt, and green pepper. Top each clam with the breadcrumb mixture, sprinkle with a dash of hot pepper sauce, and place under broiler until golden brown.

Mussels á L'escargot

Courtesy of the National Aquaculture Association

(www.thenaa.net)

Ingredients:

40 U.S. farm-raised mussels
½ cup dry white wine

Snail Butter:

½ cup unsalted butter, softened
2 tablespoons parsley, chopped
2 cloves garlic, minced
1 tablespoon lemon juice
Pinch salt
Pinch ground white pepper
½ cup breadcrumbs

Directions:

Rinse the mussels with cold water. Steam the mussels in the white wine in a covered pot for 5-7 minutes or until the shells have opened. Once they start to open, stir the mussels so that all of them open (discard any mussels that do not open). Remove from heat.

Snail Butter:

Cream the butter, chopped parsley, minced garlic, lemon juice, salt, and white pepper. Mix well so the ingredients are evenly dispersed. Remove the mussels from their shells. Place one mussel in each half shell, discarding the other shell. Dot the mussels with snail butter. Sprinkle breadcrumbs on top. Place under the lowest setting on the broiler until the butter is melted and the breadcrumbs are golden brown.

Note: Farm-raised mussels tend to have a milder flavor than wild stocks and since they are grown suspended in the water, they tend to have less grit.

Linguine with Clams

Courtesy of the National Aquaculture Association

(www.thenaa.net)

Ingredients:

2 teaspoons olive oil
50 U.S. farm-raised littleneck clams
2 cloves garlic, chopped
½ cup white wine
1 cup chicken stock
6 tablespoons butter
1 pound linguine, cooked
16 grape tomatoes, cut in half
1 tablespoon parsley, chopped
Salt and pepper, to taste

Directions:

Heat olive oil in a large frying pan. Add garlic and clams and cook until garlic turns golden. Add wine, stock, and butter. Add cooked linguine, tossing constantly until sauce starts to reduce and clams open (discard any clams that don't open). Add cherry tomatoes, parsley, salt, and pepper to taste.

Codfish with Spicy Tomato Sauce

Courtesy of the North Atlantic Marine Alliance

(www.namanet.org)

Ingredients:

4-6 pounds cod steaks/fillets
5 tablespoons cooking oil
1½ teaspoons salt
½ teaspoon cayenne pepper
½ teaspoon ground turmeric
1 teaspoon whole fennel seeds
1 teaspoon whole black mustard seeds
2 medium onions, peeled and coarsely chopped
2 cloves garlic, peeled and finely chopped
2 teaspoons ground cumin seeds
2-3 teaspoons sugar
1 (1 lb.) can chopped tomatoes, with juice
¼ teaspoon garam masala

Directions:

Rub the fish with 2 tablespoons oil, ½ teaspoon salt, ¼ teaspoon cayenne pepper, and turmeric. Cut the cod into medium-sized steaks or use fillets. Broil, grill, or bake the fish until it is done, about 5 minutes on each side. Heat 3 tablespoons oil in a saucepan over medium heat. Add mustard seeds and fennel seeds to hot oil. When the mustard seeds begin to pop after a few seconds, add onions and garlic. Stir-fry the onions over a low heat until the onions turn slightly brown, about 20 minutes. Add the ground cumin seeds, 1 teaspoon salt, sugar, and ¼ teaspoon cayenne pepper and fry for 3 minutes. Add tomatoes (with juice) and garam masala. Bring to a boil. Cover and simmer gently for 30 minutes. Serve the sauce on the side with fish.

Note: You can use this sauce for any white fish. Salmon also goes well. The sauce can be refrigerated for 3-4 days.

Simple Shrimp and Garlic Sauté

Courtesy of Nina MacDonald, Toronto Garlic Festival
(www.torontogarlicfestival.ca)

Ingredients:
6 medium-sized shrimp
¼ cup canola oil
4 cloves garlic, minced
1 teaspoon kosher salt
Freshly ground black pepper, to taste
1 tablespoon clarified butter

Directions:
Combine shrimp, oil, garlic, salt, and pepper in a bowl. Gently stir to combine ingredients. Cover and set in the refrigerator overnight. Heat a non-stick or seasoned skillet to low or medium heat. Add butter. When a few drops of water dance in the pan, add the shrimp. Cook until pinkish red. Additional garlic may be added one minute before serving (don't let the garlic burn).

Serve with lemon wedge.

Note: This recipe makes two side dish servings. By using more shrimp, it can be served as a main course. Prawns or shrimp can be used.

Meat & Poultry Entrées

Turkey and Kiwifruit Pasta Salad

Serves 8

Ingredients:

½ cup wine vinegar
2½ tablespoons olive oil
2 tablespoons Dijon mustard
2 teaspoons basil
1 large clove garlic, minced
1 (8 oz.) package spiral noodles
2 cups broccoli florets
2 cups sliced crookneck squash
4 kiwifruit
1 pound cooked turkey breast, sliced
1 cup red pepper strips
½ cup sliced green onions
⅛ cup grated Parmesan cheese

Directions:

Combine vinegar, oil, mustard, basil, and garlic; mix well. Cook noodles as package directs. Add broccoli and squash to the last 30 seconds of cooking the noodles and drain. Pour dressing over noodles, and allow to cool. Peel and slice kiwifruit. Toss turkey, red pepper, green onions and kiwifruit with pasta. Sprinkle with Parmesan cheese to serve.

Turkey-Apple Gyros
Serves 4

Ingredients:

1 medium Golden Delicious apple, cored and thinly sliced
2 tablespoons fresh lemon juice
1 cup thinly sliced onion
1 medium red bell pepper, cut into thin strips
1 medium green bell pepper, cut into thin strips
1 teaspoon olive oil
8 ounces cooked turkey breast, cut into thin strips
6 whole wheat pita bread rounds, lightly toasted
½ cup plain low-fat yogurt
1 clove garlic, minced

Directions:

Toss apple with lemon juice; set aside. In a large non-stick skillet, sauté onion and peppers in hot oil, stirring frequently until crisp-tender. Add turkey to skillet and stir until heated through. Stir in apple mixture. Add garlic to yogurt and mix. Fold pitas in half and fill with turkey mixture. Drizzle with yogurt mixture.

Turkey Burgers with Cilantro Pesto

Serves 4

Ingredients:

1 pound ground turkey
½ cup chopped onion
1 jalapeño pepper, seeded and minced
¼ cup prepared chunky salsa
1 clove garlic
½ teaspoon oregano
½ teaspoon salt
4 hamburger buns, split and toasted
Cilantro Pesto (see page 47)

Directions:

In medium bowl, combine turkey, onion, jalapeño, salsa, garlic, oregano, and salt. Evenly divide mixture and shape into four burgers, approximately 4½ inches in diameter. Grill burgers over medium-high heat for 5 to 6 minutes per side until meat thermometer registers 160°F to 165°F and meat is no longer pink in the center. To serve, place cooked burgers on bun bottoms; top with 2 tablespoons Cilantro Pesto (see page 47) and bun tops.

Cilantro Pesto

Makes ⅔ cup

Ingredients:

1 clove garlic
1 cup cilantro leaves
¼ cup walnuts, chopped
¼ cup Parmesan cheese, grated
¼ teaspoon salt
¼ cup olive oil

Directions:

In a food processor, fitted with a metal chopping blade, with motor running, drop 1 clove garlic through feed tube to finely chop. Add 1 cup packed cilantro leaves, ¼ cup each chopped walnuts and grated Parmesan cheese, and ¼ teaspoon salt; process 45 to 50 seconds or until smooth, scrape down sides of bowl. With motor running, slowly add ¼ cup olive oil and process until well blended. Cover and refrigerate several hours.

Potatoes with Leeks and Chicken

Serves 8

Ingredients:

2 tablespoons olive oil
3 cloves garlic, minced
2 tablespoons chopped, fresh ginger root
2 teaspoons curry powder or to taste
½ teaspoon crushed, dried chilies
¼ teaspoon allspice
¼ teaspoon cinnamon
3 leeks, trimmed and chopped
3 potatoes, peeled and cut in 1-inch chunks
1 cup low-sodium tomato sauce
2 cups low-sodium chicken broth
3 cups butternut squash, peeled and cubed
2 red peppers, diced
4 chicken breasts, boned

Directions:

Heat oil in large saucepan or Dutch oven. Add garlic, ginger, spices, and leeks. Cook a few minutes until tender. Add potatoes, tomato sauce, and chicken broth. Cook 10 minutes. Add squash and peppers; cook 15 minutes or until vegetables are tender. Lightly brush chicken breasts with oil. Grill approximately 10 minutes on each side, or until juices run clear. Cut each chicken breast into 3 or 4 large pieces and add to sauce. Reheat just before serving. Sprinkle with cilantro.

Spanish Hot Dish Dinner

Serves 6

Ingredients:

¾ pound ground turkey meat
1 cup chopped onion
2 garlic cloves, minced
1 (14½ oz.) can no-added-salt whole tomatoes, undrained and chopped
1 (4 oz.) can diced green chilies, drained
⅓ cup raisins
½ teaspoon salt
½ teaspoon pepper

½ teaspoon cinnamon
¼ teaspoon cloves
¼ teaspoon allspice
¼ teaspoon nutmeg
¼ teaspoon orange rind
½ teaspoon hot sauce
1 cup canned black beans, rinsed and drained
2 cups finely chopped apple
3 cups cooked brown rice
Non-stick cooking spray

Directions:

Cook turkey meat over medium heat until browned, stirring to crumble. Drain any juices and pat dry with paper towels and set aside. Wipe drippings from skillet and coat with cooking spray; place over medium heat until hot. Add onion and garlic; sauté 2 minutes or until tender. Return turkey meat to skillet. Add tomatoes, green chilies, raisins, salt, pepper, spices, orange rind, and hot sauce. Bring to boil, then reduce heat to simmer, uncovered, for 15 minutes. Add beans and apple. Cook for 10 minutes, stirring occasionally. Serve over rice.

Spanish Paella

Serves 4

Ingredients:

2 tablespoons olive oil
1 medium onion, diced
1 clove garlic, minced
1 cup rice (dry)
1 cup diced red pepper
¾ cup diced zucchini
2½ cups low-sodium chicken broth
¾ cup frozen peas, thawed
1 (14 oz.) can tomatoes, no sodium added
1 (15 oz.) can chickpeas, rinsed and drained
⅛ teaspoon salt
⅛ teaspoon pepper
⅛ teaspoon saffron
1 pound peeled shrimp

Directions:

Heat olive oil in oven-safe large skillet. Add onion and garlic. Stir for 3 minutes on medium heat. Add rice, red pepper, zucchini, and ½ cup of chicken broth. Stir for another 5 minutes. Add remaining ingredients, except shrimp. Stir and place skillet in oven. Bake at 375°F for 20 minutes. Add shrimp. Cook until shrimp turns pink, about 5 minutes.

Mandarin Stir-Fry Beef

Serves 4

Ingredients:

8 ounces beef top sirloin or top round steak, cut into bite-sized strips

¼ cup juice from tangerines (1 to 2)

2 tablespoons hoisin or oyster sauce

1 tablespoon lite soy sauce

2 cloves garlic, minced

½ cup low-sodium chicken or beef broth

1½ cups broccoli flowerets

⅓ cup sliced green onion

4 cups sliced Chinese or Napa cabbage

1 (8 oz.) can sliced water chestnuts, drained

2 tangerines, peeled, segmented

Hot cooked rice

Directions:

Remove any excess fat from steak strips; place in shallow non-metal dish. In small bowl, stir together tangerine juice, hoisin sauce, soy sauce, and garlic. Pour mixture over meat; toss to coat. Cover and chill 30 minutes to several hours. Drain meat, reserving marinade. In a wok or large skillet over high heat, place 3 tablespoons broth. Stir-fry broccoli 3 minutes. Remove from wok. Add more broth if needed; stir-fry onion and cabbage for 2 minutes. Remove from wok. Add more broth if needed; stir-fry water chestnuts and tangerines for 1 minute. Add meat and cooked vegetables back into wok, along with reserved marinade. Toss well; cover and heat 1 minute. Serve with hot rice, cooked in unsalted water.

Chicken Mole with Vegetables

Serves 6

Ingredients:

3 pounds chicken drumsticks and thighs, skin removed
3 cups canned reduced-sodium chicken broth
6 dried guajillo chilies, seeded
6 tomatillos, husks removed, washed and chopped
1 onion, chopped
5 cloves garlic, peeled
2 teaspoons ground cumin
3 cups water
4 chayotes, peeled and chopped
¾ pound green beans, trimmed

Directions:

Place chicken and broth in a large pot. Bring to a boil over
high heat. Reduce heat to medium-low. Simmer, uncovered, for
30 minutes. In a large pan, cook chilies over low heat, turning
frequently, until they change color and become fragrant. Stir
in tomatillos, onion, garlic, cumin and 1 cup water. Bring to a
boil over high heat. Cook, uncovered, for 5 minutes. Remove
pan from heat. Let cool. Place chili-tomatillo mixture (mole) in
a blender container. Puree until smooth. Return pureed mixture to pan. Cook over medium heat, stirring occasionally, until
thickened, about 5 minutes. Stir the thickened mole into chicken
and broth. Simmer, uncovered, for 15 minutes. Meanwhile, in a
medium saucepan, bring 2 cups water to a boil over high heat.
Add chayotes and green beans. Cook 5 minutes. Drain. Serve
with chicken and mole.

Potato and Pork Curry

Serves 4

Ingredients:

1 teaspoon olive oil
1 medium onion, cut in wedges
2 cloves garlic, minced
2 teaspoons curry powder
1 (14 oz.) can tomatoes
1 (14 oz.) can no-salt-added green beans, drained
4 potatoes (medium-sized), cooked and cut in chunks
2 cups cubed or strips cooked pork
⅓ cup seedless raisins

Directions:

Place onion, garlic, curry, and oil in 2-quart casserole dish. Microwave on high for 2 minutes. Stir. Add tomatoes and green beans. Microwave on high 4 minutes, stirring after 2 minutes. Add potatoes, meat, and raisins. Mix well. Microwave on high 2 minutes or until hot. Season with salt and pepper, if desired.

Vegetable and Chicken Stir-Fry
Serves 6

Ingredients:
Sauce:
3 tablespoons low-sodium soy sauce
1 tablespoon rice vinegar or cider vinegar
2 teaspoons sesame oil
2 teaspoons cornstarch

Stir-Fry:
¾ pound boneless, skinless chicken breasts, cut in thin strips
2 cloves garlic, minced
2 teaspoons vegetable oil
10 cups fresh or frozen vegetables of your choice (such as broccoil florets, snow peas, shredded cabbage, chopped bell pepper, chopped jicama, chopped onion, or sliced mushrooms)
Rice

Directions:
Sauce:
In a small bowl, mix sauce ingredients together.

Stir-Fry:
In a large skillet or wok, stir-fry chicken and garlic in hot oil until browned. Add vegetables, cover, and cook 5 minutes (longer if vegetables are still frozen), stirring occasionally. Cook until vegetables are tender but still crisp. Stir in sauce; cook until sauce thickens. Serve over warm rice.

Hot Hot Freezer Meatballs

Courtesy of the Garlic Seed Foundation
(www.garlicseedfoundation.info)

Ingredients:

1 egg

1 large head garlic cloves, peeled

1 small onion, sliced

¼ cup hot sauce (or less for less "heat")

1 pound lean ground beef

¾ cup quick cooking oatmeal

½ cup grated Parmesan cheese

1 teaspoon coarse ground black pepper

½ teaspoon salt (optional, cheese adds saltiness)

½ teaspoon Italian seasoning herbs (or ½ teaspoon each chopped fresh basil and oregano)

Directions:

Pre-heat oven to 400°F. Combine egg, garlic, onion, and hot sauce in a blender or food processor. Pour over meat in large bowl. Add the remaining ingredients and mix well with your hands. Scoop out 1-inch balls with melon baller or spoon onto large non-stick cookie sheet. Bake at 400°F for 15 minutes or until done. Time may vary depending on the size of meatballs and size of cookie sheet. Do not overcook or they will be too dry. Cool slightly, then pour off any fat, and/or drain meatballs briefly on paper towel. Cool completely; divide into meal-size portions for freezing.

Note: These make a versatile and quick meal in pasta or spaghetti sauce, in a quick sauce to put over potatoes, or in stir-fried vegetables (especially mixes of garlic and mushrooms).

Shepherd's Pie

Courtesy of Hood River Garlic Farm

(www.hoodrivergarlic.com)

Serves 4

Ingredients:

Pie:

1½ pounds organic ground beef

1 medium onion

2 carrots, peeled and chopped

1 tablespoon chopped garlic

1 tablespoon rosemary

½ cup chicken or beef stock

1 red or green pepper, chopped

1 tablespoon flour

Salt and pepper, to taste

Crust:

7 medium potatoes, chopped

½ cup whole milk

3 tablespoons butter

3 tablespoons garlic

Directions:

Pie:

Pre-heat oven to 400°F. Heat ground beef in a skillet for about 10 to 12 minutes over medium heat, until cooked. Drain off fat. Combine onions, carrots, garlic and rosemary. Add chicken or beef stock and simmer about 12 minutes until carrots are tender. Add green pepper. Let all the soup stock evaporate, and mix in the flour. Make sure filling is moist but not too wet, drain off liquid if needed.

Pour the pie mixture into an 8- x 13- by 2-inch deep baking dish. Set aside while preparing the crust mixture.

Crust:

Bring two quarts of water to a boil. Add potatoes and boil until tender. Add salt if desired. In a small skillet melt butter over low heat. Add garlic and stir frequently until the garlic is lightly brown. Drain off the potatoes, and transfer back into pot. Add milk and garlic and blend with mixer until all the lumps are gone. Salt and pepper to taste. Spread mashed potatoes over the meat mixture, making sure to cover the whole pie filling. Bake for 20 minutes, until crust is golden brown.

Garlic Burgers

Courtesy of Hood River Garlic Farm

(www.hoodrivergarlic.com)

Serves 4

Ingredients:

5 or 6 large cloves garlic

1 pound beef

Salt and pepper, to taste

Directions:

Chop garlic cloves. Light and pre-heat grill. Place your chopped garlic in a large bowl and add the ground beef. Mix the garlic into the beef by hand and form into patties, evenly distributing the garlic into the beef. Place patties on grill and allow to fully cook.

Chicken Chili

Courtesy of Hood River Garlic Farm
(www.hoodrivergarlic.com)
Serves 8

Ingredients:

¼ cup extra-virgin olive oil
½ cup chopped onion
5 garlic cloves, pressed
1 large Anaheim pepper,
chopped with seeds removed
2 jalapeño peppers, chopped
with seeds removed
3 tablespoons chili powder (up
to 4 tablespoons)
1 tablespoon cumin
2 (35 oz.) cans stewed
tomatoes, crushed (see black
bean recipe on page 59)

2 tablespoons tomato paste
¾ cup chicken stock
1 bag homemade black beans,
thawed
1 teaspoon dried oregano
4 cups shredded, cooked
chicken meat
Salt and pepper, to taste
Shredded cheddar cheese,
cilantro and sour cream, for
garnish

Directions:

In a large sauce pan, add olive oil and onions. Cook over med-high heat, stirring frequently, until golden, about 5 minutes. Add garlic, peppers, chili powder, cumin and sauté for 3 minutes. Add more olive oil if needed. Add tomatoes, tomato paste, stock, black beans, oregano, salt, pepper, and cooked chicken meat. Bring mixture to a simmer and reduce heat to low. Simmer, uncovered, for an hour, stirring frequently. Salt and pepper to taste.

Homemade Black Beans

Courtesy of Hood River Garlic Farm
(www.hoodrivergarlic.com)
Makes about 12 cups

Ingredients:

1½ pounds dry organic black beans
½ cup onion
1 tablespoon minced garlic
3 tablespoons organic molasses
1 teaspoon cinnamon
Salt and pepper, to taste

Directions:

The night before you want to make your beans, rinse the black
beans well (be on the lookout for tiny foreign objects mixed in
the beans, like small rocks!). Place the rinsed beans in a crock
pot, fill with enough water to cover the beans (at least 1½
inches over the beans), and let sit over night. In the morning
drain off the water and rinse again. Cover the beans with water
again. Add the onion, garlic, salt, and pepper. Cover the crock
pot and turn on high. Cook about 4 hours, stirring regularly.
After the first 4 hours, test a bean to check for doneness. You
can now turn the crock pot on low and continue to stir regularly
until the beans are soft (they will probably take about 4 more
hours on low). When they are cooked completely, turn off crock
pot and stir in the molasses and cinnamon. Allow beans to sit
until cooled. Set aside your 2 cups for the chili recipe (see page
58) and freeze the rest.

Vegetarian Entrées

Bow Tie Pasta with Roasted Garlic and Eggplant

Serves 6

Ingredients:

1 (12 oz.) package dried large bow tie pasta
2 tablespoons fresh parsley
¼ cup freshly grated Parmesan cheese
1 bulb garlic, roasted
6 cups eggplant, peeled and cut into 1-inch cubes
½ cup balsamic vinegar
4 tablespoons olive oil
¼ teaspoon dried oregano
½ teaspoon fresh ground pepper
3 cups (about 3 medium) chopped tomatoes

Directions:

Separate roasted garlic cloves, peel, and set aside. In a medium bowl, combine eggplant, vinegar, 3 tablespoons olive oil, oregano, and pepper. Mix thoroughly and marinate in the refrigerator for 1 hour. Place eggplant mixture, with liquid, on a baking pan. Bake in a pre-heated 425°F oven for 25 minutes. Stir every 5 to 6 minutes. About 10 minutes before eggplant is completely cooked, heat 1 tablespoon olive oil in a skillet. Add tomatoes and garlic. Sauté for 5 minutes. At the same time, cook pasta in a pot of boiling water according to package instructions. Drain and divide cooked pasta on 4 serving plates. Cover pasta with roasted eggplant. Cover with equal portions of tomato-garlic mixture and top with parsley. Serve immediately sprinkled with Parmesan cheese.

Spanish Pesto Pasta

Serves 4

Ingredients:

8 ounces fettuccine
1 tablespoon olive oil
1 garlic clove, minced
3 cups fresh spinach, stems removed
1 cup fresh basil leaves, stems removed
½ cup vegetable broth, low-fat, low-sodium
¼ cup grated Parmesan cheese

1 (15 oz.) can cannellini beans, rinsed and drained
1 cup chopped red bell pepper
1 teaspoon black pepper

Directions:

Cook pasta as directed on package. Drain and place in large mixing bowl. In a blender, add olive oil, garlic, spinach, basil, Parmesan cheese, and vegetable broth. Mix well until leaves are blended. Pour sauce over pasta. Mix until pasta is well coated. Add beans and red bell pepper. Lightly toss and serve.

Pasta Fagioli
Serves 8

Ingredients:
2 tablespoons olive oil
1 cup chopped onion
2 cloves garlic, minced
2 (14.5 oz.) cans no-salt-added stewed tomatoes, undrained
1 (15 oz.) can low-sodium vegetable broth
3 cups water
1 (15 oz.) can cannellini beans, drained
1 (15 oz.) can red kidney beans, drained
1 cup diced green pepper
¼ cup chopped fresh parsley
1 teaspoon basil leaves
¼ teaspoon black pepper
½ teaspoon oregano
1 teaspoon rosemary
4 ounces uncooked small shell pasta

Directions:
Heat oil in large pot or Dutch oven over medium heat until hot; add onion and garlic. Cook until onion is translucent. Stir in tomatoes with liquid, broth, beans, parsley, basil, pepper, oregano, and rosemary. Bring to a boil, stirring occasionally, and then reduce heat to low. Simmer, covered, for 10 minutes. Add pasta and simmer for 10 to 12 minutes until pasta is tender. Serve immediately with whole-wheat bread and side salad.

Papaya Black Beans and Rice

Serves 6

Ingredients:

2 teaspoons olive oil
1 cup chopped red onion
½ cup orange juice
¼ cup lemon juice
2 tablespoons fresh chopped cilantro
½ teaspoon cayenne pepper
1 cup finely chopped red bell pepper

1 cup finely chopped green bell pepper
1 medium papaya, peeled, seeded, and diced
2 garlic cloves, minced
2 (15 oz.) cans black beans, rinsed and drained
6 cups hot cooked brown rice

Directions:

Heat oil in large skillet over medium heat. Add all ingredients except beans and rice. Cook for 5 minutes, stirring occasionally, until bell peppers are crisp-tender. Stir in beans. Cook about 5 minutes or until heated through. Serve over rice.

Black Bean, Pasta, and Artichoke Heart Medley

Serves 12

Ingredients:

1 tablespoon olive oil
1 cup sliced green onions
½ teaspoon oregano
½ teaspoon basil
¼ teaspoon salt
⅛ teaspoon black pepper
⅛ teaspoon cayenne pepper
1 garlic clove, minced
2 (14.5 oz.) cans no-salt-added whole tomatoes, undrained and chopped
1 (15 oz.) can black beans, rinsed and drained
4 cups hot cooked pasta (any shape)
1 (14 oz.) can artichoke hearts, drained and quartered

Directions:

Heat oil in a large, non-stick skillet over medium heat. Add green onions and sauté 5 minutes. Add oregano, basil, salt, peppers, garlic, and tomatoes; cover and simmer 10 minutes. Add beans; cover and simmer an additional 5 minutes. Combine bean mixture, hot cooked pasta, and artichoke hearts in a large bowl. Toss well. Serve warm or at room temperature.

Mexican Casserole

Serves 6

Ingredients:

4 ounces uncooked ziti pasta
2 medium onions, chopped
1 garlic clove, minced
2 medium carrots, finely chopped
1 green pepper, chopped
1 medium zucchini, chopped
1 (16 oz.) can no-salt-added tomatoes, undrained
1 (8 oz.) can no-salt-added tomato sauce

1 teaspoon oregano
1 (16 oz.) can black beans, rinsed and drained
1 (10 oz.) package frozen corn, thawed
2 tablespoons green chilies, chopped
8 ounces fat-free ricotta cheese
4 ounces shredded, low-fat Monterey Jack cheese
Non-stick cooking spray

Directions:

Cook ziti according to package directions without salt; drain well. Pre-heat oven to 375°F. Coat a Dutch oven or large pot with cooking spray. Add onions, garlic, carrots, peppers, and zucchini; sauté over medium heat for 10 minutes, stirring often. Stir in tomatoes, tomato sauce, and oregano. Bring to a boil; reduce heat to low, simmering 15 minutes. Stir in beans, corn, chilies. Cook for 5 minutes. Remove from heat; add pasta and cheeses, tossing gently. Spoon into a 9-inch square baking dish coated with cooking spray. Bake for 30 minutes or until heated through. Let stand 5 minutes before serving.

Mexibean Mock Lasagna

Serves 6

Ingredients:

2 teaspoons olive oil
1½ cups chopped onion
3 garlic cloves, minced
1 green pepper, coarsely chopped
1 red pepper, coarsely chopped
1 teaspoon ground cumin
2 teaspoons chili powder spice blend
⅛ teaspoon cayenne powder
1 cup frozen or fresh corn kernels
1 (15 oz.) can dark red kidney beans, rinsed and drained

1 (15 oz.) can black beans, rinsed and drained
1 cup no-salt-added tomato sauce
1 (4 oz.) can diced green chilies, drained
6 corn tortillas
1 cup fat-free ricotta cheese
¾ cup low-fat cheddar cheese, shredded
Non-stick cooking spray

Directions:

In large skillet, heat oil over medium high heat. Sauté onion, garlic, and peppers for 5 minutes. Stir in spices and sauté 1 additional minute. Remove from heat. Mix in corn, beans, tomato sauce, and diced green chilies. Spray 13 x 9-inch dish with cooking spray. Place 3 tortillas in the dish, arranging to cover the bottom. Spoon in half of the corn mixture, and spread ½ cup ricotta cheese on top. Sprinkle with half of the cheddar cheese. Repeat layers, using up all the ingredients. Cook, uncovered, at 350°F for 45 minutes, until casserole is thoroughly heated and cheddar cheese has melted. Let stand 5 minutes before serving.

Lemon Bulgur and Chickpea Pilaf

Serves 6

Ingredients:

1 cup medium grind bulgur
2 cups vegetable stock
1 teaspoon ground cumin, divided
1 tablespoon olive oil
1 small onion, chopped.
1 small green bell pepper, chopped
3 cloves garlic, minced

2 cups canned chickpeas, rinsed and drained
⅓ cup fresh lemon juice
⅓ cup fresh lemon juice
1 cup fresh chopped parsley

Directions:

Place bulgur in a bowl. Bring stock to a boil, add half the cumin, and pour stock over bulgur. Stir once and let sit 10 to 15 minutes, until most of the liquid has been absorbed and bulgur is fluffy. Heat oil in a heavy non-stick skillet over medium heat. Sauté onion, green pepper and half the garlic 3 to 5 minutes, stirring, until onion is translucent. Add remaining garlic and cumin. Sauté about 30 seconds. Stir in bulgur and chickpeas. Stir together a few minutes. Then add remaining ingredients, combine well and season with salt and pepper to taste. Serve hot.

Okra with Rice and Beans

Ingredients:

½ cup chopped onions

2 cups chopped tomatoes

1 teaspoon sesame oil

1 cup sliced okra

2 cloves garlic, chopped

½ cup vegetable low-sodium vegetable broth

2 cups cooked brown rice

1 cup black beans, canned

Directions:

In a medium-sized saucepan, sauté the onions and tomatoes in the oil for 5 minutes. Add the okra, garlic, and broth. Cook for 15 to 20 minutes. Serve hot over the rice and beans.

BBQ Lentils
Serves 8

Ingredients:

12 ounces barbeque sauce

3½ cups water

1 pound dry lentils

2 green peppers, diced

2 red peppers, diced

2 small onions, diced

1 clove garlic, minced

Directions:

Combine all ingredients in a slow cooker. Cover and cook on low for 6-8 hours.

Spicy Potato Balls

Courtesy of the Garlic Seed Foundation
(www.garlicseedfoundation.info)

Ingredients:

2 pounds very small, new potatoes (or potato balls cut with melon baller from large old potatoes)
2 tablespoons cooking oil
1 large head garlic, cloves peeled and coarsely crushed
2 tablespoons fresh ginger root, chopped finely
1 small onion, sliced and separated into rings
1 tablespoon curry powder (more or less as desired)
1 tablespoon lemon or lime juice
½ cup water
Salt, to taste

Directions:

Steam potatoes until just tender. Heat oil and sauté onion, garlic and ginger until soft. Add curry, sauté for 1 minute; add water, lemon/lime juice, and potatoes. Simmer a few minutes to reheat potatoes and blend flavors. Any leftovers will reheat nicely the next day.

Roasted Garlic and Winter Vegetables

Courtesy of Hood River Garlic Farm

(www.hoodrivergarlic.com)

Ingredients:

1 pound carrots, peeled

1 pound parsnips, peeled

1 large sweet potato, peeled

1 small butternut squash (about 2 pounds) peeled and seeded

1 bulb garlic, peeled (see note)

4 tablespoon extra-virgin olive oil

1 teaspoon sea salt

½ teaspoon fresh, ground black pepper

2 tablespoons chopped, fresh, flat-leaf parsley

Directions:

Pre-heat oven to 425°F.

Cut the carrots, parsnips, sweet potato, and squash into 1- to 1¼-inch cubes (don't cut too small because they will shrink). Peel garlic but do not chop.

Place vegetables into a large bowl, drizzle with olive oil, salt, and pepper; toss well. Transfer onto two sheet pans. Bake for 25-35 minutes, turning after the first 15 minutes.

Test for doneness when all vegetables are tender. Sprinkle with parsley. Serve hot.

Note: A marbled purple stripe (like Siberian) or a porcelain (like Zemo) work well because of their large cloves.

Pizza with Sautéed Peppers, Onion and Garlic Scapes

Courtesy of Hood River Garlic Farm

(www.hoodrivergarlic.com)

Makes two pies

Ingredients:

Dough:

3 tablespoons yeast (one packet)

1½ cups warm water

3 tablespoons olive oil

¼ cup white flour

¼ cup whole-wheat flour

1 teaspoon salt

Toppings:

1 tablespoon extra-virgin olive oil

½ cup onion, diced

½ cup green pepper, diced

½ cup garlic scapes (about 6 scapes), cut into ¼-inch pieces

1 tablespoon flour

1 tablespoon corn meal

2 cups organic marinara sauce

2 cups shredded mozzarella cheese

¼ cup fresh basil, chopped into thin slices

Crushed red peppers, to taste

Directions:

Pre-heat oven to 400˚F.

In a sauce pan over medium heat, add olive oil. Allow oil to heat up. Add onions, peppers and scapes to oil. Sauté for five minutes, stirring frequently.

Cook until tender. Set aside. Prepare your pizza dough

Place 1 tablespoon flour on small dish and roll pizza dough onto flour, then toss with fists. Put corn meal on pizza stone or cooking sheet. Carefully lay out pizza dough on stone. Add one cup marinara, one tablespoon at a time, evenly spreading over dough. Add one cup mozzarella, evenly spreading over marinara. Add half of garlic scape mixture, evenly spreading over cheese. Top with half the basil. Place in pre-heated oven for 18 to 22 minutes. Test center of pie for doneness. Remove from oven and transfer to cutting board. Let cool for 2 to 3 minutes before slicing. Garnish with crushed red peppers.

Dough:

To prepare dough, place yeast in large mixing bowl and add warm water to dissolve, stir in olive oil. In another bowl, mix the salt and flours together and then knead them into the yeast mixture. Cover bowl with a towel and let rise for 30 to 40 minutes. Repeat using other half of ingredients.

Crustless Lower-Fat Quiche

Courtesy of The Organic Center (www.generationsoforganic.org)
and Sara Snow (www.sarasnow.com)

Ingredients:

3 small heads organic broccoli
6 organic eggs
1 cup organic half-and-half
½ cup organic cottage cheese
½ cup plain organic Greek yogurt
3 cloves of garlic, crushed
¼ teaspoon nutmeg
¼ teaspoon cayenne pepper, plus additional for the top
½ teaspoon salt
1½ cups organic cheddar cheese
¼ cups grated organic Parmesan cheese

Directions:

Preheat oven to 375°F and lightly grease a 9-inch deep-bottomed pie pan.

Slice the broccoli into small flowers and steam until bright but still firm, then blanch in cold water to stop the cooking process. In a large bowl, whisk the eggs until smooth. Add in the half-and-half, cottage cheese, yogurt, garlic, nutmeg, cayenne pepper, and salt. Whisk or stir well until completely blended. Pour the egg mixture into your pie pan. Evenly distribute the broccoli around the pan then sprinkle the cheeses on top. Add extra cayenne pepper on top, to taste. Bake in a 375°F oven for 45-50 minutes or until set and lightly browned.

Remove from the oven and allow to set for 20 minutes.

Serve with a side of lightly dressed greens.

Note: The crust on a quiche can be delicious, but it adds extra fat and carbohydrates. If you prefer your quiche with a crust, simply prepare a standard piecrust made of whole-wheat flour in a 9-inch pie pan. Pre-bake your crust for 35-45 minutes, until lightly browned.

This recipe is for a vegetarian broccoli and garlic quiche, but it can easily be customized with added ham, sun-dried tomatoes, or other ingredients.

Five-Ingredient Spaghetti Sauce

Courtesy of Peter McClusky, Toronto Garlic Festival

(www.torontogarlicfestival.ca)

Serves 4

Ingredients:

2 tablespoons extra-virgin olive oil

1 green bell pepper, blackened on the grill or under the broiler, seeded and chopped

5-6 pounds tomatoes, preferably locally-grown plum or another not-too-juicy variety, chopped

6 cloves minced garlic

2 tablespoons minced fresh thyme leaves

1 teaspoon kosher salt

Freshly ground black pepper, to taste

Directions:

In a large saucepan add the oil, bell pepper, tomatoes, four of the garlic cloves, thyme, salt, and pepper. Bring to a boil, reduce heat, and simmer for at least 10 minutes or up to 1 hour (the longer it cooks, the thicker it gets). Add the two remaining cloves and cook for one minute longer. Serve over pasta with fresh mozzarella or any other cheese of your liking, and garlic bread.

Note: For a hearty breakfast, generously drizzle leftover sauce on a poached egg and top with Parmesan cheese.

Roasted Garlic Grilled Cheese Sandwich

Courtesy of Peter McClusky, Toronto Garlic Festival
(www.torontogarlicfestival.ca)

Makes 1 sandwich

Ingredients:

1 tablespoon roasted garlic puree
(see recipe for Roasted Garlic Spread on page 97)
2 slices whole-wheat or multi-grain bread
2 slices cheddar, American, or Swiss cheese
1 tablespoon unsalted butter or any low-fat substitute

Directions:

Spread roasted garlic on a single side of one slice of bread. Place the cheese between the slices of bread so that the roasted garlic spread is on the inside. Spread butter on the outside of the sandwich and place in pan pre-heated to medium heat. When one side is golden, turn the sandwich and cook until light brown.

Slice sandwich in half and garnish with a pickled garlic scape.

Note: Garlic scapes are delicious when pickled and can be served as a garnish with sandwiches or chopped and added to a salad or stir-fry.

Side Dishes
& Snacks

Okra and Green Beans
Serves 6

Ingredients:

1 pound okra, uncut
1 pound fresh green beans
1 cup water
1 (6 oz.) can tomato paste
1 tablespoon olive oil
1 medium onion, diced
2 large garlic cloves, crushed then chopped
½ teaspoon salt
½ teaspoon ground pepper

Directions:

Wash okra pods, trim stems, do not remove caps. Rinse well and drain. Wash beans and cut into 3-inch lengths. Combine water, tomato paste, olive oil, onion, garlic, salt and pepper in a sauce pan and mix well. Heat, stirring frequently, until mixture comes to boil. Add okra and beans and additional water, if necessary, to almost cover vegetables. Cook until okra and green beans are tender.

Winter Squash and Kale Risotto with Pine Nuts

Serves 4

Ingredients:

2 teaspoons olive oil

1 cup diced yellow onion

3 cloves garlic, minced

1 cup Arborio or short-grain rice

2 tablespoons pine nuts

2 (10 oz.) cans low-sodium, fat-free vegetable broth

1 (12 oz.) package frozen winter squash, thawed slightly and diced

2 cups finely chopped fresh kale

Directions:

Heat oil in a large, shallow saucepan over medium heat. Add salt, onion, and garlic and sauté 2 minutes. Stir in rice and pine nuts and toast for about 2 minutes, stirring occasionally. Add ½ cup broth; cook on medium-low heat, stirring often, until liquid is nearly absorbed. Add remaining broth in the first can, ½ cup at a time, stirring often until each addition is nearly absorbed before adding the next. Add diced squash, and from the second can, ½ cup of broth. Stirring often. Add remaining broth, ½ cup at a time as before. Along with the last ½ cup of broth, add the kale. Cook mixture until all broth is absorbed and kale is soft and bright green.

Pear Brown Rice

Serves 6

Ingredients:

3 tablespoons lemon juice
2 teaspoons finely chopped garlic
¼ teaspoon ground ginger
¼ teaspoon ground, black pepper
2 pears, diced
3½ cups cooked brown rice
½ cup chopped green onions
½ cup diced celery
3 tablespoons vegetable oil

Directions:

In a small bowl, combine lemon juice, garlic, ginger, and black pepper. Add pears to the mixture and set aside. In a large bowl, combine brown rice and remaining ingredients. Gently fold in pears. Serve immediately or chill in the refrigerator.

Rosemary Potato Skewers

Serves 4

Ingredients:

4 medium red potatoes (about 1⅓ pounds) peeled and cut into
1½-inch chunks
1 tablespoon olive oil
2 teaspoons butter, melted
1 tablespoon chopped, fresh rosemary or 1 teaspoon dried
rosemary
1 large clove garlic, minced
½ teaspoon salt
¼ teaspoon ground black pepper
4 (12-inch) skewers (metal or bamboo), soaked in warm water
for 30 minutes

Directions:

Prepare a charcoal grill or pre-heat broiler. In a heavy saucepan with tight-fitting lid, cook the potatoes in 2 inches of boiling
water until tender, approximately 15 minutes. Drain potatoes;
cool slightly and thread onto skewers. In a small bowl, mix
together remaining ingredients. Place potato skewers on the grill
3 to 4 inches above the glowing embers. Brush the skewers with
the rosemary mixture. Grill, basting and turning several times,
until the potatoes are lightly browned, approximately 10 to 12
minutes.

Roasted Celery with Apples
Serves 4

Ingredients:

1 large clove garlic, crushed
2 tablespoons olive oil
1 stalk celery, about 1½ pounds
2 Golden Delicious apples, cored and quartered
1 cup apple juice
¼ teaspoon ground cinnamon
¼ teaspoon salt
⅛ teaspoon ground black pepper
4 slices toasted Italian bread

Directions:

Pre-heat oven to 375°F. Place garlic and oil in a 13- x 9- x 2-inch baking pan; bake until oil is hot, about 5 minutes. Meanwhile trim base of celery; cut celery stalk crosswise, about 7 inches from base (save top for soups, stews, etc); cut stalk lengthwise into 4 wedges. Place celery, apples, apple juice, cinnamon, salt and pepper in baking pan; bake, uncovered, until celery is crisp-tender, about 40 minutes, basting with pan juices every 10 to 15 minutes; discard garlic. Serve immediately over Italian bread.

Roasted Radishes and Root Vegetables

Serves 4

Ingredients:

3 medium sweet potatoes, peeled and cut into 2-inch chunks
(about 3 cups)
4 medium parsnips, peeled and cut into 2-inch chunks
(about 2 cups)
2 medium red onions, peeled and quartered
12 ounces radishes
1 whole head of garlic, cut in half lengthwise
2½ tablespoons olive oil
½ teaspoon black pepper
1 tablespoon fresh or 1 teaspoon dried thyme
¼ teaspoon salt

Directions:

Pre-heat oven to 450°F. In a large bowl put potatoes, parsnips, onions, radishes, and garlic. Toss with olive oil, salt, and pepper. Arrange vegetables in a single layer in a 15½- x 10½-inch roasting pan. Bake until vegetables are tender and golden, stirring occasionally, about 45 minutes. Arrange vegetables on serving platter. Sprinkle with thyme and garnish with thyme sprigs if desired.

Vegetable Curry
Serves 8

Ingredients:

2 pounds mixed vegetables
(French beans, carrots, peas,
potatoes and cauliflower)
2 onions, chopped
10 mild red chilies
10 teaspoons poppy seeds
7 cloves garlic
½ teaspoon turmeric
1-inch piece fresh ginger root,
grated

3 teaspoons melted butter
½ teaspoon curry powder
7 ounces plain yogurt
3 tablespoons whipped cream
1 teaspoon sugar
Salt, to taste

Directions:

Prepare and cook the mixed vegetables according to their type,
breaking or cutting large ones into bite sized pieces. Grind the
onions, chilies, poppy seeds, garlic, turmeric and ginger to a
paste. Melt butter in a heavy based saucepan. Add the paste and
cook for 3 to 4 minutes. Stir in the curry powder and cook for a
further few minutes. Then add the vegetables and water. Bring
to a boil and cook for a few minutes. Stir in the yogurt, cream,
sugar, and salt, heat gently then serve hot with pita bread.

Autumn Vegetable Succotash
Serves 8

Ingredients:
¼ cup olive oil
1 cup diced onion
2 cloves garlic, finely chopped
2 cups diced red bell peppers
2 cups diced zucchini
2 cups diced yellow summer squash
3 cups frozen lima beans
3 cups fresh or frozen corn kernels
2 tablespoons coarsely chopped fresh sage

Directions:
In a skillet over medium-high heat, heat oil. Add onion; cook until translucent, about 2 minutes. Add garlic, bell peppers, zucchini, squash, lima beans, and corn. Season as desired; cook, stirring, until vegetables are tender, about 10 minutes. Stir in sage, and serve.

Baba Ghanoush (Eggplant Dip)

Serves 8

Ingredients:

2 large eggplants (1¼ pounds)
2 tablespoons tahini
4 cloves garlic, peeled and crushed
½ cup diced onion
1 cup chopped tomato
3 tablespoon fresh lemon juice or more to taste

4 tablespoons cold water
¼ teaspoon salt
⅛ teaspoon freshly ground black pepper
½ teaspoon olive oil
Parsley sprigs, to garnish (optional)

Directions:

Pierce the eggplants in several places with a toothpick or fork. Wrap each eggplant in aluminum foil and place on a gas grill or in the oven at 500°F. Cook until the eggplants collapse and begin to release a lot of steam, about 10-15 minutes. Remove the foil and place the eggplants into a bowl of cold water. Peel while eggplants are still hot and allow them to drain in a colander until cool. Squeeze pulp to remove any bitter juices and mash the eggplant to a puree. In a food processor, mix tahini, garlic, onion, tomato, lemon juice, and water until mixture is concentrated. With the blender running, add the peeled eggplant, salt, pepper, and olive oil. Serve in a shallow dish and garnish with black pepper, tomatoes, and parsley.

Artichoke Gondolas

Serves 4

Ingredients:

4 medium-sized artichokes, cooked
½ cup sun-dried tomatoes (not oil-packed)
1 small eggplant, peeled and diced
2 cups low-sodium chicken broth
¼ cup chopped onion
1 tablespoon fresh oregano
1 tablespoon fresh basil
2 cloves garlic, minced
¼ teaspoon pepper

Directions:

Halve artichokes lengthwise; remove center petals and fuzzy centers of artichokes. Remove outer leaves of artichokes; reserve. Trim out hearts and chop finely. Set aside. Rehydrate tomatoes in boiling water for 3 minutes until softened. Drain and rinse; chop. Cook eggplant in simmering chicken broth for 10 minutes; drain well. In blender or food processor container, place chopped tomatoes, drained eggplant, onion, herbs, garlic, salt, and pepper. Cover and process until nearly smooth. Taste for seasoning. Stir in chopped artichoke hearts. To serve, arrange artichoke leaves on a serving platter; spoon 1 heaping teaspoon of the eggplant mixture onto wide end of artichoke leaves. Garnish with a fresh herb leaf, if desired. Alternate serving idea: Arrange artichoke leaves on a platter, surrounding a bowl of the eggplant mixture. Use artichoke leaves to scoop up individual servings of the dip. Dip can be prepared up to 24 hours ahead and chilled until serving time.

Cucumber Yogurt Dip
Serves 6

Ingredients:

2 large cucumbers, peeled, seeded, and grated
2 cups plain low-fat yogurt
½ cup non-fat sour cream
1 tablespoon lemon juice
1 tablespoon fresh dill
1 garlic clove, chopped
1 cup cherry tomatoes
1 cup broccoli florets
1 cup baby carrots

Directions:

Peel, seed, and grate one cucumber. Slice other cucumber and set aside. Mix yogurt, grated cucumber, sour cream, lemon juice, dill, and garlic in a serving bowl. Chill for 1 hour. Arrange tomatoes, cucumbers, broccoli, and carrots on a colorful platter. Serve with cucumber dip.

Pickled Garlic

Courtesy of the Garlic Seed Foundation
(www.garlicseedfoundation.info)

Ingredients:

5 cloves garlic
½ cup pickling salt
4 cups cracked ice
5 cups sugar
5 cups vinegar
1½ teaspoons turmeric
½ teaspoon cloves
2 tablespoons mustard seed
2 tablespoons celery seed
6 (pint-sized) canning jars and lids

Directions:

Peel garlic, sprinkle with salt. Bury garlic in 4 cups cracked ice.
Cover with heavy plate. Let stand 3 hours to overnight, then
drain. Combine garlic, sugar, vinegar, turmeric, cloves, mustard
seed, and celery seed in a pan and bring to a boil. Meanwhile,
sterilize canning jars and lids in boiling water. Pour garlic and
liquid mixture into hot jars and seal. Let sit for at least one
month.

Greens and Beans

Courtesy of the Garlic Seed Foundation
(www.garlicseedfoundation.info)

Serves 4

Ingredients:

1 pound dandelion greens (any type of greens can be used, but bitter greens taste best)

6 (or more) garlic cloves, crushed

3 tablespoons olive oil

1 (15-16 oz.) can white beans plus juice (cannelini, kidney, navy, or Northern)

Salt and pepper, to taste

Directions:

Sauté greens, garlic, and olive oil until greens are well wilted and tender. Then add beans, smashing about ¼ of the beans. Heat through.

Note: This is an excellent side dish for chicken, pork, or fish. It is also good by itself with a hunk of homemade bread.

Salsa Fresca

Courtesy of Hood River Garlic Farm
(www.hoodrivergarlic.com)

Ingredients:

3 medium ripe tomatoes or tomatillos, cut into small pieces
1 small onion, sliced into small pieces
4 garlic cloves, chopped
4 jalapeño or Serrano chilies, chopped
¼ cup chopped cilantro
1 tablespoon fresh lime juice
¼ teaspoon salt
⅛ teaspoon oregano
Black pepper, to taste

Directions:

Place all ingredients into a Cuisinart or mini chopper and mix until blended. Serve chilled with chips or on your favorite Mexican dish.

Roasted Garlic
(3 ways to roast garlic)
Courtesy of Hood River Garlic Farm
(www.hoodrivergarlic.com)

Ingredients:
Garlic
Olive oil
Salt
Pepper

Directions:

On the Barbeque:
Select some nice big bulbs with large cloves. (Siberian makes an excellent choice because the cloves are so big.) Cut off the tips so the cloves are exposed. Wrap with aluminum foil so the tips are pointing up keeping foil loose for seasoning. Drizzle some olive oil on the exposed cloves and salt and pepper to taste. Now wrap the foil tightly around the bulb. Place on the grill over medium heat and cook for twenty minutes. Test for doneness by squeezing with a pair of tongs. The garlic is ready when the bulb is soft and can be squeezed with the tongs.

In a Terra Cotta Garlic Roaster:
Pre-heat oven to 350°F. Take three or four large bulbs and cut the tips off exposing the cloves. Drizzle with olive oil then shake salt and pepper over them. Place in oven at 350°F and bake for twenty minutes. Use a pair of tongs to squeeze the bulbs to test for softness. Garlic is done when it is soft.

In a Cast Iron Pan:

This is a great way to roast lots of loose cloves of garlic in the oven. Pre-heat oven to 350°F. This preparation requires the cloves to be peeled first, so peel about ¼ pound of cloves and place in a small cast iron pan. Sprinkle with olive oil and salt and pepper to taste. Place in oven and bake for twenty minutes. Test by piercing with a fork

Serve:

When they are done, slice a baguette lengthwise and lightly toast on the top shelf of the BBQ. Spread the garlic on the baguette by squeezing the clove. It should spread as if being squeezed from a tube. They can also be added to potatoes.

Garlic Butter and Garlic in Olive Oil

Courtesy of Hood River Garlic Farm
(www.hoodrivergarlic.com)

Ingredients:
Butter:
1½ cups butter
1 cup crushed garlic (or more, up to ½ cup)

Olive Oil:
½ cup extra-virgin olive oil
⅓ cup crushed garlic (or more, to taste)

Directions:
Butter:
Mash garlic cloves in mini chopper and mix into soft butter. Add chives, parsley and salt if desired. Form into logs, wrap in waxed paper, and place in freezer bags or plastic wrap. Store in freezer and slice as needed.

Olive Oil:
Crush the garlic as you would with the garlic butter. Then evenly distribute the crushed garlic into the bottom of a zip lock bag. Add enough olive oil to completely cover all the crushed garlic and blend gently by rubbing the outside of the bag. Freeze and slice as needed.

Roasted Garlic Spread with Sweet or Savory Toppings

Courtesy of Peter McClusky, Toronto Garlic Festival
(www.torontogarlicfestival.ca)
Makes 6 appetizers

Ingredients:

20 garlic cloves, skin left on
2 tablespoons olive oil
½ teaspoon kosher salt
1 teaspoon freshly ground black pepper

Puree:

1 tablespoon olive oil
1 teaspoon thyme
Kosher salt and freshly ground black pepper, to taste

Directions:

Pre-heat oven to 325°F. Place garlic cloves on baking sheet or casserole dish and drizzle with oil, salt, and pepper. Gently stir ingredients so that the oil coats each clove. Cover with aluminum foil or a lid and bake at 325°F for 30 minutes to one hour (depending on the size of the garlic cloves). To check for doneness, a fork should easily pierce the garlic.

Remove from oven and allow to cool for ten minutes. To remove the flesh from the cloves, hold each clove and press gently, squeezing the flesh through the sprouting end of the clove. Some parts of the clove may be a deep golden brown, due to caramelization of the sugars in the clove during cooking. Take care to include this part.

Puree:

Place roasted garlic, olive oil, and thyme in a food processor and mix for 30 seconds or until desired consistency is achieved. Alternatively, a potato masher can be used instead of a processor. Add salt and pepper to taste.

Serve on crackers or toasted baguette slices. This spread can also be accompanied with an assortment of savory toppings such as goat cheese, mozzarella, or gruyère cheese, along with thinly sliced roasted bell pepper, sun-dried tomatoes, olives, or capers. Suggested sweet toppings include pure peach marmalade, mango chutney, or brandied plum jam.

Note: This roasted garlic spread can also be used as a base in soup (such as Flu Fighter Garlic Soup on page 24), in sandwiches (such as Roasted Garlic Grilled Cheese Sandwich on page 78), or as a condiment on a baked potato.

Resources

Cornerstone Garlic Farm
www.localharvest.org/cornerstone-garlic-farm-M6792

Earthbound Farm
www.ebfarm.com

Garlic Seed Foundation
www.garlicseedfoundation.info

Generations of Organic
www.generationsoforganic.org

Hood River Garlic Farm
www.hoodrivergarlic.com

National Aquaculture Association
www.thenaa.net

North Atlantic Marine Alliance
www.namanet.org

Sara Snow
www.sarasnow.com

Toronto Garlic Festival
www.torontogarlicfestival.ca

Also in the *Farmstand Favorites* Series:

Farmstand Favorites: Apples
978-1-57826-358-5

Farmstand Favorites: Berries
978-1-57826-375-2

Farmstand Favorites: Cheese & Dairy
978-1-57826-395-0

Farmstand Favorites: Maple Syrup
978-1-57826-369-1

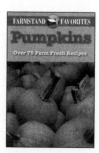

Farmstand Favorites: Pumpkins
978-1-57826-357-8